Cody's Rocky Adventure

by Carol Peske

illustrated by Rowan Barnes-Murphy

Scott Foresman
is an imprint of

PEARSON

Glenview, Illinois • Boston, Massachusetts • Mesa, Arizona
Shoreview, Minnesota • Upper Saddle River, New Jersey

Illustrations
Rowan Barnes-Murphy

Photographs
Every effort has been made to secure permission and provide appropriate credit for photographic material. The publisher deeply regrets any omission and pledges to correct errors called to its attention in subsequent editions.

Unless otherwise acknowledged, all photographs are the property of Pearson Education, Inc.

16 © Lori Adamski Peek/Getty Images

ISBN 13: 978-0-328-39352-7
ISBN 10:   0-328-39352-5

Cody walked along the beach with his head down. He was looking for rocks with his Aunt Janet. They had almost filled their bucket.

Soon they would head back to Aunt Janet's little house. Aunt Janet would get the paints and brushes, and then they would get to work.

They spent hours painting rocks.
They painted flowers and ladybugs on
some rocks. They painted silly faces on
others. Then they added the rocks to the
other painted rocks that lined the paths
around Aunt Janet's house. It was a
wonderful sight.

Cody was always unhappy when his week at Aunt Janet's was over. His mom came to pick him up, and they returned to the city on the train. It was so boring at home. There was nothing to do. Then Mom had an idea.

"Let's walk down to the new library," she said. "Today is the grand opening."

Cody liked that idea. He grabbed his book bag, and off they went.

Cody could see the new library as they got closer. It looked very unfriendly. There were no trees or flowers yet, just dirt and sidewalks. It needed some grass and plants. It also needed some color.

Just then, Cody's mom recognized someone she knew. While she visited with her friend, Cody kicked some rocks around in the dirt. The rocks reminded him of being at Aunt Janet's house. Then an idea popped into Cody's head. When his mom was finished talking, he told her his idea.

"Mom, do you know the rocks I paint with Aunt Janet?" asked Cody.

"Yes," said Cody's mom. "They look beautiful around her house."

"Maybe we could paint rocks for the library," said Cody. "Then we could place them along the sidewalks like at Aunt Janet's."

"It would take a lot of rocks," said Cody's mom, "and lots of people."

"My friends would help," said Cody.

"Let's go inside and find someone to talk to about your idea," said Mom.

Cody and his mom went inside and told the man at the desk about Cody's idea. The man said that they should tell Cody's idea to Ms. Peterson, who worked at City Hall. He gave them her phone number.

When Cody and his mom got home, his mom called Ms. Peterson. Ms. Peterson told Cody's mom that there would be a meeting the next day about how to decorate the outside of the library. She said that anyone could come to the meeting with ideas.

The next day, Cody and his mom took the bus to the meeting. Cody took with him some rocks he had painted. Cody and his mom waited for their turn to speak at the meeting. Cody's mom told everyone about Cody's idea, and Cody showed them the rocks. Then a woman spoke to Cody.

"That's a very original idea, Cody," she said. "Do you think you could get other children to help paint rocks?"

"Yes," said Cody. "It's fun, and kids like to have fun!"

"Thank you, Cody," the woman said with a smile. "We'll talk about your idea and let you know what we decide."

When Cody and his mom got home,
Cody sat and waited for the phone
to ring.

"Cody, I doubt that they are going
to call today," Mom said. "Go and play
until dinner."

The next day, the phone rang after
lunch. Cody's mom answered it and
spoke to someone.

When his mom hung up, she said, "Cody, the city thinks the painted rocks are a great idea."

"They do?" cried Cody.

"Yes, they want us to get started right away," Mom said. "The city will get the rocks."

"We have to get paints and lots of brushes," Cody said, "and lots of painters."

When Cody told the nice man at the art store about the library project, the man gave them paints and brushes for free. Then Cody told his friends about the painting project. All his friends told their families and friends.

On the first day of painting, more than fifty children were there to help! The adults helped set up. There were painting tables and drying tables.

Cody was busy painting a rock when he felt a tap on his arm. He turned around and was surprised to see Aunt Janet.

"Thank you for giving me this idea," Cody said.

"This was all your idea," said Aunt Janet. "I just came to help!"

"Sometimes big ideas come from little people," Mom said, smiling proudly at Cody.

"Would you please start to place the dry rocks, Aunt Janet?" Cody asked. "You're good at that."

"Yes, sir," said Aunt Janet. "I'll get to work."

Two weeks later, Cody and his mom were at the library again. Now it looked like a friendly place. The painted rocks added color and gave people something to look at. Grass and trees had been planted. Cody's mom led him to a new sign in front of the library.

"Can you read the sign?" Cody's mom asked.

"*Cody's Rock Garden*," Cody said with a smile.

"The library wanted to thank you for all you accomplished, so they had this sign made," said Cody's mom.

Cody felt very proud.

Kid Power

Real kids like Cody make a difference by putting their ideas to work. One girl started a group that plants trees to help the environment. Another girl started a group that collects pennies to protect police dogs. A boy started a group that gives books to children. Here is how you can make a difference too.

1. Think about what is important to you. Some ideas might be animals, the environment, other kids, or your town.

2. Choose one thing that you think you could do to help others.

3. Start small. Make a simple plan.

4. Get others to help you.